MANAGING YOUR METRON

Discover the Original   *Design of Vocation*

A STUDY GUIDE

Contents

PREFACE

"I believe that one of
the next great moves
of God is going to be
through the believers
in the workplace."

—

BILLY GRAHAM,
IN LATE 2000

Welcome to the Metron Manager Project!

This project is all about equipping you to become who you were originally designed to be and find your place in the Kingdom of God.

God has given me a vision to be part of what many believe is the next great move of God by launching the Metron Manager Project. I have been fully engaged in the cause of Christ and His Kingdom enterprise for over 25 years. As such I have gained wide experience and perspective on the trajectory of the modern mission effort. As a missionary kid I grew up primarily outside the USA in remote and developing countries. After embracing my own call to serve in missions I began working in the socially and economically devastated regions of the former Soviet Union in the early to mid 1990's. From there I participated in or led missional efforts from Southeast Asia to South America and from Europe to Africa covering 60 countries.

I've seen the edges of heaven and walked in the streets of hell. I've seen the power of God transform lives and nations through average believers like myself who have chosen to hear and obey. I believe that we are entering a new era of mission in spiritual history. This era is marked by the missionizing of believers in the marketplace. 'On mission' is the new mode of every believer in every sphere of society. My book, *Managing Your Metron*, launched this Metron Manager Project with the aim of providing a reformational understanding of Work, Mission, and Meaning.

The vision of the Metron Manager Project is to provide training, resources, and theology that will recover the dignity and mission of vocation. Billy Graham's prescient statement about the next move of God coming through believers in the workplace is a vision of the future that I and many others believe has now arrived. It is time to rethink mission and the Kingdom of God as a new era is upon us. Spiritual history is demanding a broadening of our understanding of what it means to respond to the Great Commission (Matthew 28:18-20). I invite you to join in this journey to become a Metron Manager and recover the dignity and mission of your vocation.

– Jonathan Nowlen

Author: *Managing Your Metron: A Practical Theology of Work, Mission and Meaning*
Founder: The Metron Manager Project

A PRAYER

As a career missionary and minister of the gospel I was often involved in efforts to help individuals discover their roles in the kingdom of God. I have come to recognize that I and many other church and ministry leaders often conducted our efforts from good intentions but imperfect understanding. As a consequence, we often caused the view of work and vocation to be denigrated in the body of Christ.

The aim of this study is to help you discover the true purpose of work, mission and meaning. As greater understanding of the kingdom has awakened, I want to offer this universal statement of repentance from church and ministry leaders for devaluing vocation as a prelude to beginning the study of Managing Your Metron.

In Repentance from Church and Ministry Leaders for Devaluing Vocation

WE CONFESS

1. We thought that the organized church was where everything was to happen and that everyone and everything was to be served in and through the church.
2. All real and valid ministries were understood to be within the church and were to be under its government and control.
3. We did not truly understand the Kingdom of God and how it was to manifest on the earth.
4. As a result, we used people to only build our churches and ministries.

If individuals could not or would not serve us in our vision for our ministries, our actions demeaned and undervalued them. We saw them as less important and mostly as sources of income.

Often these people were ignored or pushed aside and as a result they moved further and further toward the door. Many left in frustration, anger and disillusionment, believing they were not spiritual enough in some undefined way. Others simply gave up trying to fit themselves into the confines of the church structure and ministries.

We attempted to make business executives into intercessors, salespeople into children's nursery workers, business administrators into Sunday school superintendents, craftsmen into janitors, administrative assistants into secretaries, and the list goes on and on.

WE REPENT

In doing so we did not honor, respect, and equip those called by God to minister in commerce, media, arts, government, social services and most other vocations and occupations outside the church walls. We are sorry.

PLEASE FORGIVE US

On behalf of many pastors and ministry leaders, we want to tell you that we have been wrong. For what we did and taught for generations in the church we are sincerely sorry. We are before you today in repentance for our bad attitudes, our wrong beliefs, and our poor behaviors toward you.

WE BLESS YOU!

We honor you as Kingdom people — called by God to the marketplace. We believe you are ordained by him to occupy and transform the sphere of influence to which he has called you.

Today, we release honor and blessing and favor on your life and personal calling to the marketplace. We are prepared to stand with you and support you in your God given ministry — outside the walls of the institutional church.

You have dreams ordained by God. It is our privilege and our hearts desire to call them forth, and to see you fully established in the destiny of God's desire for your life.

FACILITATORS

Thanks so much for your willingness to lead other believers through this curriculum. Each session covers several chapters of the book Managing Your Metron and is divided into five sections.

REVIEW

Use the bullet points to guide the group in a review of the recommended reading.

Try this interactive approach in reviewing the key points:

- Ask any group member to state the answer to the 'blank' in bullet points below.
- When the correct answer is voiced, everyone can then fill in the blank with the correct answer.
- If no answer is given, ask a group member to look up the statement on the indicated book page and share it with the group.
- If working with a larger group, consider breaking up into smaller groups of 3 to 4 people.

Once all the blanks have been filled in, ask the group if there were any key points that were:

- Totally new concepts or ideas to them.
- Difficult for them to agree with, and if so, why?

DISCUSSION

Guide your group in discussing these focus questions. You can do them in any order you like and don't feel like you need to get through them all. If other good questions come up related to today's session, then just flow with it!

APPLICATION

This section brings focus to the personal application of key concepts covered in this session. Ask participants to individually consider the questions and make notes. If appropriate, invite participants to share their findings. If working with a larger group, consider breaking up into smaller groups of 3 to 4 people.

TAKEAWAY

Your group can work together to identify their key takeaways or participants can do so individually.

PRAYER

This is a time for personal prayer and reflection guided by the points listed here. If appropriate, invite participants to share any key insights God revealed to them regarding their key takeaways.

Made to Matter *Chapter 1*

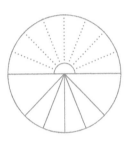

Review
20 MIN

"The Spirit Himself testifies with our spirit that we are children of God, and if children, heirs also, heirs of God and fellow heirs with Christ." (Romans 8:16-17)

1. In the kingdom being saved _____ is also being saved _____.

   (page 3)

2. As one who is born again, you receive _____ citizenship and begin to

   manage a _____-_____ identity. (page 3)

3. You have inherited the _____ of God, but that inheritance comes with

   _____. (page 4)

4. _____ is not just to get you through the door of heaven, but it is to get

   _____ onto the earth through you. (page 4)

5. Our _____ in the kingdom is defined by embracing a life of

   _____ with Christ and taking personal _____ for creation.

   (page 4)

Called to Work *Chapter 2*

"The heavens are the heavens of the Lord, But the earth He has given to the sons of men." (Psalm 115:16)

1. We are all responsible for _____ a sphere of influence in God's created order — the call to _____ is the call _____ . (page 5)

2. This call to work is not to earn _____ but to _____ with God to align creation with his original _____ . (page 5)

3. All of creation is _____ waiting for you to _____ your calling and get to work! (page 5)

4. God has called us to _____ with him in the _____ business. (page 5)

5. Our _____ are part of the _____ to the Lord's Prayer, "Your kingdom come, your will be done, on earth as it is in heaven." (page 6)

Designed to Shine *Chapter 3*

"...you will shine among them like starts in the sky..." (Philippians 2:5)

1. The Kingdom is _____ when you shine according to your _____ . (page 10)

2. You shine when you radiate the _____ - _____ of Jesus in the midst of the ashes and brokenness of the _____ around you. (page 10)

3. Our desire to shine does not emanate from our _____ nature but our _____ design (page 9)

4. Knowing one's _____ is the rudder that guides our boat through the _____ we experience all around us on this fast-moving river of life. (page 10)

5. Every follower of Christ must understand that their _____ is vital in seeing his _____ come and his will be done. (page 10)

Kingdom Context *Chapter 4*

"The coming of the Kingdom of God is not something that can be observed, nor will people say, 'Here it is,' or' there is it,' because the Kingdom of God is in your midst [within you]." (Luke 17:20-21)

1. By _____ to the King, you are under his _____ and you can, in turn, receive delegated authority to _____ the King. (page 13)

2. No _____ force can alter your inner kingdom position unless you step out from under the _____ of the King and submit to the wrong lord. (page 14)

3. The kingdom always functions from the _____ to the _____ . (page 15)

4. From within the _____ of the believer, the kingdom is released outward as influence _____ by authority. (page 15)

5. The kingdom is all about _____ internal transformation, not _____ modification. (page 15)

1. If a Christian knows they have been saved from sin but does not recognize they have been called to co-labor with God, how are their thoughts, speech and actions affected?
2. What are the implications of believers being called to co-labor with God in establishing His Kingdom on the earth? How would the Church be different if every believer started to take responsibility and walk in this truth?
3. What are some common phrases or language used in the body of Christ that might be out of alignment with God's original design for vocation?

Discussion
30 MIN

NOTES

_____
_____
_____
_____
_____

_____

_____

_____

_____

_____

_____

_____

_____

Application

20 MIN

Religion and politics say, "Submit, behave & comply." The Kingdom of God says, "Believe, behold & transform."

1. Identify an area of your metron that you have been trying to change (e.g. stopping an unhealthy habit; restoration of a broken relationship; financial restoration).

2. What have you been doing to try to effect change in that area of your metron?

3. Have your efforts been focused on behavior modification or internal transformation?

4. How could you change your approach to orientate yourself with the Kingdom model of internal transformation?

NOTES

_____

_____

_____

_____

_____

_____

_____

_____

_____

_____

Identify your key takeaways from today's session. What will be the two or three things that you will focus on until the next session?

1. _____

2. _____

3. _____

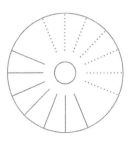

Takeaway
5 MIN

1. Ask God what He is excited to co-labor with you on in your life.

2. Ask God to highlight specific areas in your life that are out of alignment with the Kingdom of Heaven.

3. Pray that God would enable each person in your group to shine in their sphere of influence.

4. Pray for your own personal transformation process and then pray for a specific transformation to happen in the world around you, in your metron.

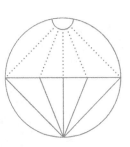

Prayer
10 MIN

CHAPTERS   SESSION 2   5 THRU 7

Gardens and Kingdoms *Chapter 5*

"Now it will come about that in the last days, the mountain of the mountain of the house of the Lord will be established as the chief of mountains, and will be raised above the hills; and all the nations will stream to it." (Isaiah 2:2)

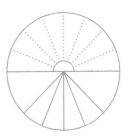

Review

20 MIN

1. From the tiny _____ of Jesus' life on earth, the kingdom is becoming the

    very _____ of God filling all of creation. (page 17)

2. There are many other "_____" or "kingdoms," but the Kingdom of God will

    overtake and _____ them all. (page 17)

3. Satan's strategy seems to be to cover up the epic _____ he suffered at the

    cross and keep people under his _____ through not allowing them to see

    the light. (page 18)

4. Though Jesus took back all _____ from the enemy and his kingdom of little

    hills at the cross, there are plenty of people who _____ the kingdom of

    darkness over the kingdom of light. (page 19)

5. Jesus moved decisively and _____ against the lesser _____

    kingdoms through his death and resurrection. (page 19)

Spiritual Sea Change *Chapter 6*

*"You are from God, little children, and have overcome them; because great-
er is He who is in you than he who is in the world."* (1 John 4:4)

1. We are living in the middle of the greatest _____ sea change in spiritual

    history, and we have the privilege to be commissioned as _____ with Christ.

    (page 21)

2. We are on a cooperative mission or co-mission with Jesus to _____ the

    works of the devil and _____ the fiefdoms of the little plants in the garden.

    (page 21)

3. Creation has again _____ access to its true _____ of life, Jesus

    Christ. (page 22)

4. You were designed and _____ to _____ the world around you.

    (page 22)

5. We now find _____ empowered with _____ authority from

    the King of Kings and Lord of Lords. (page 23)

The Great Dissipation *Chapter 7*

*"...they think it strange that you do not run with them in the same
flood of dissipation, speaking evil of you."* (1 Peter 4:4)

1. We live in a world of ever-increasing _____ . (page 25)

2. We must have a compelling _____ which empowers us to constrain or

    "focus" our _____ to reach our potential. (page 25)

3. _____ the only alternative to life in the kingdom - you either focus or you

    fade. (page 25)

4. Acting on the understanding that you are designed with purpose is the only

    _____ to the cultural _____ that kills the soul and pulls

    _____ away from the kingdom. (page 27)

5. Unless we find our _____ and calling in the kingdom, we become content

   to _____ responsibility for the condition of the world around us. (page 27)

1. Are you surprised to learn there is competition for your loyalty between the kingdom of this world and the Kingdom of Heaven?

2. Do you see a cultural drift in the body of Christ today? If so, in what ways?

3. In what ways can Christians use their God given authority to take responsibility for the world around them?

Discussion
30 MIN

NOTES

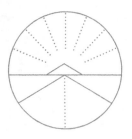

1. Do you feel like you are focusing or fading in your life?

2. Are there areas in your life that seem more loyal to darkness than to light?

3. What is the compelling vision that empowers you to focus?

4. In what ways are you using the authority God has given you to take responsibility for the world around you?

Application

20 MIN

NOTES

_____

_____

_____

_____

_____

_____

_____

_____

Identify your key takeaways from today's session. What will be the two or three things that you will focus on until the next session?

1. _____

2. _____

3. _____

Takeaway

5 MIN

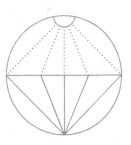

1. Ask the Lord to help you choose to submit to the right Kingdom in every area of life.

2. Ask God to reveal any works of darkness in your own heart or actions and repent for partnering with the wrong kingdom.

3. Pray for heavenly perspective so you can expose the works of darkness around you and ask God what to do about them.

4. Ask God to help you to hear and respond to what he is calling you to do so you can focus and not dissipate.

Prayer
10 MIN

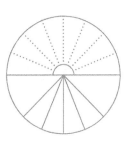

The Original Design *Chapter 8*

"Now no shrub of the field was yet in the earth, and no plant of the field had yet sprouted, for the Lord God had not sent rain upon the earth, and there was no man to cultivate the ground." (Genesis 2:5)

1. The software of _____, combined with the hardware of _____, created a perfect "operating system." (page 29)

2. By _____, this operating system _____ heaven and earth. (page 29)

3. It was God's original design that mankind would be both _____ and _____ in their created nature. (page 29)

4. His original design required a _____ relationship with _____ to operate the system that he had created. (page 30)

5. The desire for _____ is hard-wired into our very being and drives much of our _____. (page 30)

6. This desire to be _____ and _____ is part of God's perfect operating system. (page 30)

"God blessed them; and God said to them, 'Be fruitful and multiply, and fill the earth, and subdue it; and rule over the fish of the sea and over the birds of the sky and over every living thing that moves on the earth.'" (Genesis 1:28)

COLABORING

1. A unique aspect of Adam and Eve's role in creation was that they were designed to manage their _____ relationship with God and manage their _____ . relationship with the rest of creation. (page 33)

2. The operating system of creation was designed to require the meaningful involvement of mankind. (page 33)

ORIGINAL COMMISSION

3. God made creation to require Adam and Eve's _____ . They had to _____ for creation to _____ . (page 34)

4. At this moment work was given _____ and connected mankind with the _____ . (page 34)

COMMISSIONED TO WORK

5. Adam's original commission was to take responsibility to see the world outside of the garden become like the world inside the garden. (page 35)

6. The theology of work can be summed up as "Work is Good—Work was _____ the Fall and is not a _____ of the Fall." (page 36)

CREATION IS WAITING ON YOU

7. When mankind doesn't cultivate or "work," then human purpose is _____ , and creation _____ . (page 37)

8. Work is the intended means by which all of mankind is to cooperate with God to subdue creation. (page 38)

WORK IS A HIGH CALLING

9. When you find calling in your _____ , then what seems to be ordinary becomes _____ . (page 39)

10. When a high view of work is embraced your vocation becomes a joy-filled, kingdom-building activity in which we co-labor with our father, God. (page 41)

CO-LABORING BY DESIGN

11. God chose to co-labor with mankind as an expression of intimacy and trust. (page 43)

12. He left room for mankind to have a very real and vital role in the management of the _____ _____ . (page 44)

Welcome to Your Metron *Chapter 10*

"We, however, will not boast beyond measure, but within the limits of the sphere [metron] which God appointed us..." (2 Corinthians 10:13 NKJV)

1. God _____ and _____ every human a metron. (page 46)

2. The metron is a measure of _____ delegated by God to you in the midst of creation, culture, and _____ history. (page 46)

3. What you do with what God has given you matters throughout _____ , starting now. (page 46)

4. Managing your metron becomes the heart of your _____ and the context within which you find _____ . (page 47)

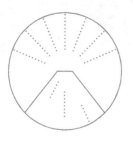

Discussion

30 MIN

1. Have you ever thought of yourself as called to co-labor with God?

2. Do you feel naturally supernatural? Or do you feel only aware of your material existence?

3. What is the most ordinary thing that you do in life that you wish was somehow extraordinary and meaningful?

4. Previous to this study, did you assume that work was a result of sin and the fall?

5. What is the true heart and purpose of any vocation?

NOTES

_____

_____

_____

_____

_____

_____

_____

_____

_____

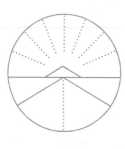

Application

20 MIN

1. What are three to five obvious areas that fall within your God given metron: (Note: Avoid over-thinking your response here. Your understanding and insights into your metron will evolve throughout this study so just write down what comes to mind at this point.)

2. Identify an area within your metron were you are facing a challenge and consider your thoughts and actions towards it. Do they reveal a victim mentality where you feel powerless to influence, or the mindset of one who knows they are called to bring order and subdue?

3. Take a moment to consider what that area of your metron would look like if you co-labored with God? How would you approach these challenges differently?

NOTES

_____

_____

_____

_____

_____

_____

_____

_____

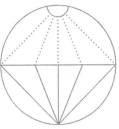

Identify your key takeaways from today's session. What will be the two or three things that you will focus on until the next session?

1. _____

2. _____

3. _____

Takeaway

5 MIN

1. If you only feel that you live naturally and can't understand God's original design for you, ask God to awaken your spirit to know that you are naturally supernatural.

2. Pray that God would show you how valuable you are in His Kingdom.

3. Repent in prayer if you feel that you have embraced a low view of work and been disconnected from your design.

4. Ask God to show you what He has given you delegated authority to influence in your metron.

Prayer

10 MIN

CHAPTERS   4   11 THRU 12

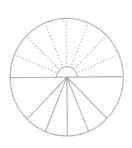

Cultivate *Chapter 11*

"Then the Lord God took the man and put him into the garden of Eden to cultivate it and keep it." (Genesis 2:15)

Review

20 MIN

1. Work includes all your areas of _____ and _____ , including family, social, and vocational activities - work is not just what you do to earn money. (page 50)

2. Your work and influence are given a particular realm that has set borders or boundaries. (page 50)

3. All that is _____ within these borders is what the apostle Paul refers to as your " _____ ." (page 50)

THE GOOD WORK OF VOCATION

4. Our father is in the _____ and _____ business, and your collaboration (co-laboring) with him is how he gets business done. (page 51)

5. No matter what you do on a day to day basis, you are commissioned to reverse the effects of the fall within anyone or anything that you can influence. (page 52)

6. In the kingdom, work can be defined as any _____ to which you set your _____ to do. (page 52)

WORLD VIEWS OF WORK

7. Animistic worldview regarding work: The distinguishing characteristic of this view is that "work is a _____ _____" that one puts up with in order to have food to eat. (page 52)

8. Materialistic Worldview of Work: The distinguishing characteristic of this view is that a person works to _____ and have _____ wealth. (page 53)

9. This sacred and secular delineation is not biblical - it was introduced through the heresy of Gnosticism. (page 53)

THE DENIGRATION OF VOCATION

10. Gnosticism is based on two false premises: _____ is inherently evil, and the _____ is inherently good; everything in (of) the body has no meaning because life only exists in the spirit realm. (page 53)

11. Gnosticism leads to a "dis-integrated" life rather than a holistically managed human existence.

12. The idea that some things in life are _____ , and some are _____ is rooted in Gnosticism and is opposed to a biblical worldview - in the kingdom worldview, everything is integrated. (page 54)

ARE YOU A CHRISTIAN GNOSTIC?

13. Two prominent Gnostic paradigms:

    i. There is work that is 'spiritual', (such as pastoring or missions), and work that is 'secular,' (which is seen as slightly evil, bad or only necessary).

    ii. One should endeavor to 'spiritualize' secular work by only seeing your workplace as a place to do spiritual ministry. (page 54)

14. The great loss of these Gnostic Paradigms is that by embracing a _____ view of work you have been dislocated from your _____ . (page 54)

15. Work is by its very design spiritual and of eternal significance - You have to work for creation to work. (page 55)

VERTICAL & HORIZONTAL CULTIVATION

1. The garden provided an _____ of what creation would be like when all was

    in _____ both spiritually and naturally or vertically and horizontally. (page

    58)

2. In the Kingdom of God you are again required to manage up and manage out. (page 58)

3. The condition of your _____ relationship will inform what you reproduce

    into your _____ environment. (page 58)

THE ORIGINAL CONNECTION

4. The garden was the original _____ _____ between heaven and

    earth, a place where it was likely hard to tell where earth ended and heaven began. (page

    59)

5. When we _____, heaven entered our _____, and we entered

    heaven. (page 59)

6. In the garden model, we see that the _____ was in _____ but

    he was ruling through _____ relationship with his people. (page 60)

ON EARTH AS IT IS IN HEAVEN

7. Now that Jesus has taken back all authority and paid the price for every sin, we can co-la-

    bor with God to reconnect _____ with its _____. (page 61)

8. Reconciliation and restoration are the _____ of the believer, and the metron

    you have received is the _____ for your work. (page 61)

9. A right relationship with God turns all of mankind's _____ into connection

    points with _____. (page 61)

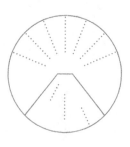

Discussion

30 MIN

1. What areas of work and responsibility do you see in your own metron?

2. Did you realize before this study that we are commissioned to work? If so, in what ways?

3. What worldview of work did you most relate to in your own life?

4. Describe the distinction of a Kingdom world view of work vs. the Evangelical Gnostic views.

5. What are you currently doing to manage up (relationship with God) and manage out (relationship to Creation) in your metron?

NOTES

_____

_____

_____

_____

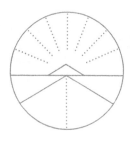

Application

20 MIN

1. Do you have a Kingdom worldview of work? When rating your agreement with the following statements, consider your thoughts, actions and speech in everyday life to help you identify your world view. *Note:"Work" includes all your areas of responsibility and influence, including family, social, and vocational activities — it is any activity to which you set your hand to do.*

Work has spiritual significance.
Strongly Disagree .... *Disagree* .... *Not Sure* .... *Agree* .... *Strongly Agree*

Work is a reflection of the character and nature of God.
Strongly Disagree .... *Disagree* .... *Not Sure* .... *Agree* .... *Strongly Agree*

God uses work as a means to establish his Kingdom on the earth.
Strongly Disagree .... *Disagree* .... *Not Sure* .... *Agree* .... *Strongly Agree*

Work is of eternal value.
Strongly Disagree .... *Disagree* .... *Not Sure* .... *Agree* .... *Strongly Agree*

Work is an act of worship.
Strongly Disagree .... *Disagree* .... *Not Sure* .... *Agree* .... *Strongly Agree*

Work is a calling from God on a person's life.
Strongly Disagree .... *Disagree* .... *Not Sure* .... *Agree* .... *Strongly Agree*

Work has inherent dignity and imparts dignity.
Strongly Disagree .... *Disagree* .... *Not Sure* .... *Agree* .... *Strongly Agree*

Work is God's original design for mankind.

Strongly Disagree ········· *Disagree* ········· *Not Sure* ········· *Agree* ········· *Strongly Agree*

Work is vital for creation to flourish.

Strongly Disagree ········· *Disagree* ········· *Not Sure* ········· *Agree* ········· *Strongly Agree*

2. Identify two of the above points where your worldview is not aligned with a Kingdom worldview.

3. What changes could you foresee in your metron if these points were aligned with the Kingdom?

NOTES

_____

_____

_____

_____

_____

Identify your key takeaways from today's session. What will be the two or three things that you will focus on until the next session?

1. _____

2. _____

3. _____

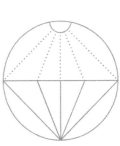

Takeaway
5 MIN

1. Ask God what He is calling you to do. What is he asking you to set your hand to?

2. Ask God to show you something within your metron that is obviously under the effects of the fall and sin. Pray for the effects of the fall to be healed in this area.

3. If you have realized that you are living and thinking like a Christian gnostic then ask God to transform your mind and re-integrate you as a whole person.

4. Ask God to guide you in how to better steward and manage your relationship upwards with God.

Prayer
10 MIN

Culture Matters *Chapter 13*

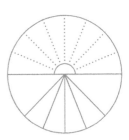

"So he was saying, "Then Jesus asked, "What is the Kingdom of God like? What shall I compare it to? It is like a mustard seed, which a man took and planted in his garden. It grew and became a tree, and the birds perched in its branches." (Luke 13:18–19)

Review
20 MIN

1. Culture is a by-product of _____ , and that culture is fundamentally

    _____ . (page 63)

2. Culture is ultimately a _____ of spiritual realities _____ with

    the context of the natural world - it is a system that is informed by whomever mankind

    _____ . (page 69)

3. People have the power and authority to _____ the garden of their

    _____ for better or worse. (page 70)

4. Culture is designed to be the primary _____ example of the

    _____ of God. (page 70)

5. Seed + God + Mankind × _____ = Kingdom (page 71)

The Formation of Culture *Chapter 14*

"And do not be conformed to this world, but be transformed by the renewing of your mind, so that you may prove what the will of God is, that which is good and acceptable and perfect." (Romans 12:2)

1. Culture is the _____ that is left in a people by whatever they worship. (page 74)

2. High culture is a _____ of the human relationship with the _____ and the garden was a living example of what the culture of heaven produced when it touched earth. (page 75)

3. The art of managing your metron is to start with the right _____ code and through your _____ ensure that its cultural system is operating on earth as things are in heaven. (page 77)

4. You become what you _____. You look like what you worship. You reproduce what you _____. (page 79)

5. You are designed to behold him and _____ his ways into your metron - this is how you can see his _____ established. (page 80)

Ruin or Restoration *Chapter 15*

"For you were formerly darkness, but now you are Light in the Lord; walk as children of Light (for the fruit of the Light consists in all goodness and righteousness and truth), trying to learn what is pleasing to the Lord. Do not participate in the unfruitful deeds of darkness, but instead even expose them." (Ephesians 5:8–11)

1. Through _____ the Lord, we are _____ into his image, but if we behold and value something other, we will become like that upon which we gaze. (page 81)

2. When we are lured away and deceived into worshiping idols of any kind, the enemy has successfully found a _____ through which he can _____ into your metron. (page 81)

3. Through the process of _____ the author of righteousness (God), we easily detect _____ code. (page 82)

4. Culture is under constant _____ between being a manifestation of the ways

of God or a manifestation of the _____ world system that is informed by the

enemy. (page 85)

5. We all have an inherent _____ to influence and influence is how your met-

ron will be _____ for better or worse. (page 85)

Metron Apostles *Chapter 16*

*"You are from God, little children, and have overcome them; because great-
er is he who is in you than he who is in the world."* (1 John 4:4)

1. You are an apostle to your metron - you establish _____ culture in the

_____ of your metron. (page 88)

2. The physical and spiritual condition of our metron constantly _____ and

flows and requires continual _____ if it is to become pleasant and welcom-

ing to the presence of God. (page 88)

3. In your God-given sphere of influence, many _____ forces are willfully

bringing _____ into the ecosystem you are managing. (page 88)

4. In the kingdom, God designed that the _____ would look like the

_____ . (page 88)

5. Today, the kingdom influencer serves as a _____ for heaven to touch earth -

the presence of God and all that originates in him is intended to _____

through you to the world around you. (page 90)

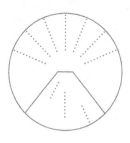

Discussion
30 MIN

1. How does your initial understanding of the nature of culture compare to what was presented in this study?

2. How can you bring the right source code to influence your metron?

3. Did you ever consider your work to be worship?

4. How does the idea of being responsible as a cultural influencer make you feel?

5. As a metron apostle, what is at least one area of the 'new territory' in the Kingdom that you can focus on to bring alignment with the culture of Heaven?

NOTES

_____

_____

_____

_____

_____

_____

_____

_____

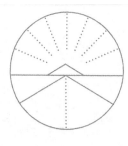

Application
20 MIN

1. Consider your sphere of influence. Is the source code that is governing your metron authored in Heaven? If not, then identify what the areas of broken code that need to be recoded.

2. If the world around you is often a reflection of the world inside you then what does the condition of your metron communicate about you?

3. What you worship (behold) becomes the source code of your metron's culture. Are there things in your metron that do not reflect Heaven's culture? If so, what are you worshiping or beholding that could be distorting your metron?

NOTES

_____

_____

_____

_____

_____

_____

_____

_____

_____

Identify your key takeaways from today's session. What will be the two or three things that you will focus on until the next session?

1. _____

2. _____

3. _____

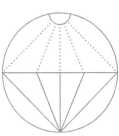

Takeaway

5 MIN

1. Ask God to show you if you have idols in your life that are shaping who you are becoming.

2. Ask God if anything inside you is blocking your connection with the Holy Spirit and limiting what He wants to do through you.

3. Pray that you would be a heavenly lens through which the wisdom and presence of God would radiate into your metron.

4. Ask God to guide you in shaping the culture in your metron.

Prayer

10 MIN

Commissioned and Recommissioned *Chapter 17*

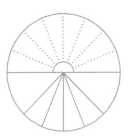

"God blessed them; and God said to them, 'Be fruitful and multiply, and fill the earth, and subdue it; and rule over the fish of the sea and over the birds of the sky and over every living thing that moves on the earth.'" (Genesis 1:28)

Review
20 MIN

1. **Original Commission:** God has always been committed to _____ with his creation and he has always chosen to do it through _____ . (page 93)

2. **Noah:** The Lord makes his point again in Genesis 9:8 by clearly telling Noah and his family that he is _____ his original _____ with mankind. (page 94)

3. **Tower of Babel:** Not only was the rebellion at Babel aligned with _____ goals but it illustrated a completely wrong understanding of God's original design for how he chooses to _____ with man.

4. Managing your metron requires you to rule _____ and serve _____ . (page 99)

The Footprint of Heaven *Chapter 18*

"He who believes in Me, as the Scripture said, 'From his innermost be-ing will flow rivers of living water.'" (John 7:38)

1. There was a three-part model clearly portrayed in the original design of cre-

    ation;_____, Eden, and the _____. (page 103)

2. There is an intriguing correlation found in scripture regarding God's manifest presence in

    the _____ and the presence of God in the _____. (104)

3. In the kingdom, points of _____ always start in a garden but are never in-

    tended to be _____. (page 104)

4. Your very _____ is now the garden temple of the _____, and

    the presence of God now flows from you like the rivers that flowed out of the Garden of

    Eden. (page 107)

5. Through co-laboring with God, you are actively working to _____ the ef-

    fects of the fall in your _____. (page 108)

Metrons Matter *Chapter 19*

"For our struggle is not against flesh and blood, but against the rul-ers, against the powers, against the world forces of this darkness, against the spir-itual forces of wickedness in the heavenly places." (Ephesians 6:12)

1. In co-laboring with Christ to manage your metron, you impart life and blessing through

    your _____, beliefs, _____, and character. (page 109)

2. Jesus said he came to _____ the works of the devil, and he gave us all au-

    thority to do likewise. (page 110)

3. Another way to think about "displacement" is to compare it with the parallel command to

    "_____" that God gives in the original commission to Adam. (page 111)

4. Kingdom influence is the manifestation of God's ways through his _____,

    your thoughts, and your _____. (page 115)

5. _____ or culture are the _____ that is co-authored by man-

kind and whichever spiritual authority with which they align — either with the one true God or with the "lesser" gods of this world. (page 115)

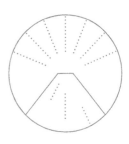

1. Does it surprise you that God is so committed to connection and restoration of relationship with all of Creation?

2. What does it look like to functionally 'rule' spiritually and 'serve' naturally?

3. If I am truly the new 'temple' of the Holy Spirit, how does that affect how I live my life?

4. Is your influence a conduit for Gods ways to be made known both in the spiritual and the natural?

NOTES

_____

_____

_____

_____

_____

_____

_____

_____

_____

_____

_____

_____

_____

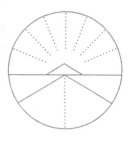

1. What are some specific action steps I can take in the natural to serve areas of my metron that need the affects of the fall reversed?

2. List 3 steps you can take to displace and destroy the works of darkness in your metron. (Note: remember that Kingdom authority always flows from inside you out to the world around you. It is influence, not imposition.)

3. List 3 examples of 'software' (ways / culture) that appear to be authored by 'lesser gods' and are operating freely in your metron.

Application
20 MIN

NOTES

_____

_____

_____

_____

_____

_____

_____

_____

_____

_____

Identify your key takeaways from today's session. What will be the two or three things that you will focus on until the next session?

1. _____

2. _____

Takeaway
5 MIN

3. _____

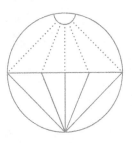

1. Ask God for the wisdom and guidance to effectively rule spiritually and serve naturally.

2. Pray that you would become an example of a Garden Temple that would bring life to the world around you.

3. What works of darkness are being exposed by God in your metron? Pray that these would be displaced by righteousness and the ways of God.

4. Pray that the 'ways' or 'culture' inside you would be rewritten to align with the software of heaven.

Prayer
10 MIN

Navigating Your Commission *Chapter 20*

"The good man out of the good treasure of his heart brings forth what is good; and the evil man out of the evil treasure brings forth what is evil; for his mouth speaks from that which fills his heart." (Luke 6:45)

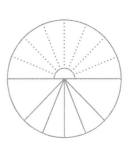

Review
20 MIN

1. We are entrusted with supervisory _____ and _____ by our heavenly father to influence his creation and carry out his purposes. (page 117)

2. The awareness that we have a _____ is deeply seated in our original design, and all of mankind has an inner _____ to shape the world around them. (page 118)

3. By taking _____ for our metron and _____ with Christ, we have nothing to lose and everything to gain. (page 118)

4. You have been _____ and positioned to _____ darkness and replace it with the light of God. (page 119)

5. The world _____ you begins to look like the world inside you, and just like your heavenly Father, your words carry _____. (page 119)

Coding Your Metron *Chapter 21*

"And many peoples will come and say, 'Come, let us go up to the mountain of the Lord, to the house of the God of Jacob; that he may teach us concerning his ways and that we may walk in his paths.'" (Isaiah 2:3)

1. There is nothing in your metron that you will not be able to manage when you follow the paths of God's _____ toward heavenly _____. (page 121)

2. The _____ of God is the source code of heaven - the soft-ware of blessing that God created to _____ his creation. (page 121)

3. The simple model outlined in Isaiah is truly the heart of God's original design for how every metron should be _____ and every garden cultivated. Go up and be taught concerning his ways, that we may walk in his paths. (page 122)

4. Your mandate is to _____ the Lord, learn the _____ wisdom of God, and then beautifully guide and shape your garden. (page 123)

5. Corrupt Code: The corrupted code or "virus" that was introduced is still being injected through _____ and has been _____ to God's original design. (page 123)

6. Fixing Code: Wisdom and understanding flow from relationship with God and empower and commission us to creatively write code according to the culture of heaven. (page 125)

7. Ultimately the kingdom project culminates when all of Christ's enemies are _____ having been subdued. The true end game is when Christ hands over the completed _____ project to the Father. (page 126)

1. What areas of darkness seem to stand out to you the most? Do you feel that you are empowered to displace these works of darkness? Why or why not?

2. Are there areas in your metron that you feel you need wisdom from God to manage?

3. What do you feel is limiting you from meeting with the Lord and doing things His way in His universe?

NOTES

_____

_____

_____

_____

_____

_____

_____

_____

Discussion
30 MIN

1. What areas of 'code' seem corrupted or dysfunctional in your metron? Ask God for a download of wisdom for His solutions and write down at least 1 possible solution you feel is prompted by the Lord.

2. Do you feel that there is anything to lose by taking responsibility to co-labor with God to manage your metron? If so, write it down:

3. Describe practically what it would look like for you to behold the Lord, learn the manifold wisdom of God, and then beautifully guide and shape your garden.

NOTES

_____

_____

Application
20 MIN

_____

_____

_____

_____

_____

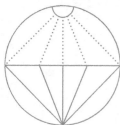

Identify your key takeaways from today's session. What will be the two or three things that you will focus on until the next session?

1. _____

2. _____

3. _____

Takeaway

5 MIN

1. Pray that God would give you understanding and wisdom regarding the spiritual authority and power that He has delegated to you.

2. Ask God to give you wisdom and understanding to seek heavenly solutions.

3. Ask God to give you the grace to hear what is on His heart for your metron.

Prayer

10 MIN

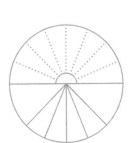

Occupy *Chapter 22*

"Then the Lord God took the man and put him into the garden of Eden to cultivate it and keep it." (Genesis 2:15)

Review

20 MIN

1. People often find that it is easier to _____ to something than to retain it - the keeping of what has been gained requires _____ . (page 128)

2. Your vocation is the means that God uses to hold the _____ of the kingdom. (page 129)

3. In the new covenant, the royal _____ still serves to cultivate worship as the connection point between heaven and earth, but now the robes become work clothes, and the rituals become _____ . (page 133)

4. Within our commission we are not only to take _____ through multiplication, subduing and cultivation but also to hold the ground. The build _____ within the kingdom does matter. (page 135)

5. Success with the qualitative often is related to managing _____ and _____ . (page 136)

6. The role of guarding, protecting, and watching over what was _____ is the bottom line of stewardship. (page 137)

"If you do not do well, sin is crouching at the door; and its desire is for you, but you must master it." (Genesis 4:7b)

7. When you manage your metron, you will find that the enemy wants to

    _____ you into _____ him. (page 140)

8. Successful _____ assurance requires us to understand our delegated author-

    ity. (page 141)

9. A spiritually _____ metron is one that has an atmosphere so filled with the

    presence of God that any darkness that slips in is naturally _____. (page 143)

10. You pursue transformation by the _____ of your _____. (page
    143)

11. Displacement and transformation are both fruits of _____ and

    _____. (page 144)

Discussion

30 MIN

1. Why do believers often feel like they struggle to maintain what they have attained in life?
2. What does your identity as a royal priest in God's Kingdom mean to you personally and to the world around you in your metron?
3. How would you describe the concept of spiritual authority if you were sharing it with another person who was a believer?
4. Is God highlighting an area of your metron that needs to become more spiritually resilient?

NOTES

_____

_____

_____

_____

_____

Use the following key indicators to evaluate your ability to keep and guard your work.

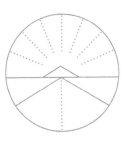

1. Do you protect the processes and practices that are at work in your metron?
    Never .... *Rarely* .... *Sometimes* .... *Often* .... *Always*

2. Is the presence of God evident in your actual work efforts?
    Never .... *Rarely* .... *Sometimes* .... *Often* .... *Always*

3. Do you watch over your source code and operating system that manages your metron?
    Never .... *Rarely* .... *Sometimes* .... *Often* .... *Always*

4. Is the culture of heaven consistently evident in you to those you influence?
    Never .... *Rarely* .... *Sometimes* .... *Often* .... *Always*

5. Do you value the quality of your work as much as the quantity of work you accomplish?
    Never .... *Rarely* .... *Sometimes* .... *Often* .... *Always*

6. Are you just as faithful with a little responsibility as you are with a lot?
    Never .... *Rarely* .... *Sometimes* .... *Often* .... *Always*

7. Do you seek Godly means as well as Godly outcomes?
    Never .... *Rarely* .... *Sometimes* .... *Often* .... *Always*

8. Do you constantly stay spiritually aware of guarding the gates to your garden?
    Never .... *Rarely* .... *Sometimes* .... *Often* .... *Always*

9. Do you endeavor to keep the rivers of living water flowing freely from within you into your metron?
    Never .... *Rarely* .... *Sometimes* .... *Often* .... *Always*

10. Do you regularly evaluate the condition of your metron against the benchmarks seen in the word of God?
    Never .... *Rarely* .... *Sometimes* .... *Often* .... *Always*

11. Do people experience a vacation in heaven when they interact with you?
    Never .... *Rarely* .... *Sometimes* .... *Often* .... *Always*

12. When you read the Bible do you see the 'ways' of God as a vital layer within the scriptures?
    Never .... *Rarely* .... *Sometimes* .... *Often* .... *Always*

13. Is your metron spiritually resilient to the level that sin and darkness are naturally repelled?
    Never .... *Rarely* .... *Sometimes* .... *Often* .... *Always*

NOTES

_____

_____

_____

_____

_____

_____

_____

_____

_____

Identify your key takeaways from today's session. What will be the two or three things that you will focus on until the next session?

1. _____

2. _____

3. _____

Takeaway

5 MIN

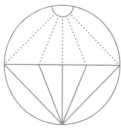

_____

1. Pray that God would give you the ability to live your vocation as a royal priest

2. Ask God to show you what areas of your Metron have been 'built' without consideration of quality and durability - where are the weak areas?

3. Pray over your personal indicators seen in the application section above.

4. Pray and repent if you feel that you have not been 'keeping' your Metron and ask God to help you retain what has been attained.

Prayer

10 MIN

CHAPTER   SESSION 9   TWENTY-FOUR

Metrons and Missions *Chapter 24*

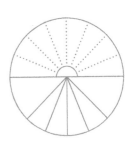

"And Jesus came up and spoke to them, saying, "All authority has been given to Me in heaven and on earth. Go therefore and make disciples of all the nations, baptizing them in the name of the Father and the Son and the Holy Spirit, teaching them to observe all that I commanded you; and lo, I am with you always, even to the end of the age." (Matthew 28:18–20)

Review

20 MIN

ON MISSION

1. First element of vocation is to _____. The second is to _____.

   The third element is to be on _____. (page 147)

2. Bringing the _____ and presence of God, into an area where it is not

   known, is by definition, _____. (page 148)

3. The _____ elements of the Great Commission might be suitably approached

   as a task, but the second element can only be fulfilled as an ongoing, open-ended way of

   _____. (page 150)

MAKE DISCIPLES WHO MAKE IT RIGHT

4. The second half of the Great Commission is all about _____ disciples to

   guard, protect, and watch over all that is commanded and all that is _____.

   (page 150)

5. There are those who are called into _____ ministry and those that are called to _____. (page 155)

6. The _____ is called and positioned in their metrons to do the work of guarding, protecting, and watching over. This majority is commissioned to _____ others how to manage their metron. (page 155)

7. When a member of the 97% is not called or compelled to emphasize the _____ function, their _____ toward being on mission continues. (page 156)

8. The quantitative and qualitative aspects are not _____ _____—the whole of each commission is given to each member of the body of Christ. (page 156)

9. No two metrons look _____ the same, and no two metrons need exactly the same sort of _____ labor. (page 156)

10. In managing your sphere of influence, the need for quantitative and qualitative work _____ and _____. (page 156)

HOLISTIC MISSION

11. Some _____ is best done by a member of the 97%—providing that the one doing the discipling understands their scriptural _____, power, and has a commission to do so. (page 157)

12. Whether you _____ with the calling of the 3% in vocational ministry or with the 97% who's ministry is vocation, all are called and commissioned—all are on _____. (page 158)

13. Missionized _____ is at the heart of kingdom expansion. (page 159)

THE MISSIONAL EDGE

14. Living "on mission" is simply doing what you can, when you can, where you can as a faithful _____ with Christ. It is simply _____ what God values and

doing what he would do. (page 164)

15. If you are to live on mission in your metron, remember you live from _____

    towards earth. (page 164)

16. Restoring the broken _____ in nations, cultures, lives, and souls is the busi-

    ness of the metron _____. (page 165)

1. Have you ever felt that you were called to be 'On Mission' but didn't know what that actu-
   ally could look like given your particular vocation? If so, in what ways?

2. Within your metron, what does it mean for you to do the qualitative work of guarding,
   protecting, and watching over what has already been cultivated?

3. Do you feel like you are managing your metron from a place of authority, seated in
   heavenly places with Christ, or are you appealing up to heaven in a reactive way due to
   circumstances?

Discussion
30 MIN

NOTES

_____

_____

_____

_____

_____

_____

_____

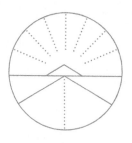

Application

20 MIN

Looking at this list of Qualitative and Quantitative aspects of being On Mission, what seems to be emphasized in your life? Put a mark on the dotted line scale between each quantitative and qualitative aspect to indicate where you feel that you are on the spectrum. Please note that this self survey does not require a binary choice but aims to provide you with a point of reference to better understand your design in the Kingdom.

QUANTITATIVE		QUALITATIVE
Reach	. . . .	Teach
Evangelize	. . . .	Disciple
Quantity	. . . .	Quality
Width	. . . .	Depth
Subdue	. . . .	Occupy
Abad (cultivate)	. . . .	Shamar (guard)
Go	. . . .	Stay
Width	. . . .	Depth
Expansion	. . . .	Permanence
Cultivate	. . . .	Keep

1. What broken edges are becoming visible within your metron?

2. What restorative solutions does God bring to your mind regarding the broken edges He is highlighting?

3. What qualitative elements in your metron do you feel you are able to influence?

4. What quantitative opportunities do you feel are being highlighted to you within your metron?

NOTES

_____

_____

_____

_____

_____

_____

_____

_____

Identify your key takeaways from today's session. What will be the two or three things that you will focus on until the next session?

1. _____

2. _____

3. _____

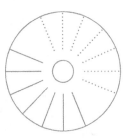

Takeaway
5 MIN

1. Ask God to form an 'On Mission' mindset within you.

2. Pray that God would show you what areas of qualitative discipleship He has positioned you to do in your metron. Who should you invest in and 'teach to observe'?

3. Ask God if He is calling you to serve as a full time vocational Christian worker in the 3%. Do you feel pulled towards a missionary or pastoral calling?

4. Ask God to empower you to guard, protect and watch over all that is in your metron and to value Work as Worship!

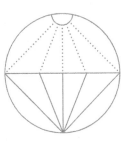

Prayer
10 MIN

CHAPTER   SESSION 10   TWENTY-FIVE

Managing Expansion *Chapter 25*

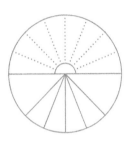

"Enlarge the place of your tent, stretch your tent curtains wide, do not hold back; lengthen your cords, strengthen your stakes. For you will spread out to the right and to the left; your descendants will dispossess nations and settle in their desolate cities." (Isaiah 54:2–3)

Review
20 MIN

1. _____ in the Kingdom of God is commissioned to _____ out,

   fill the earth, and subdue it. (page 167)

2. Managing _____ is part of the job description for metron managers - it is

   the _____ of being on mission. (page 168)

3. _____ is the _____ work of every believer. (168)

4. God's activities are visible to all - but understanding his _____ comes from a

   place of trusted, intimate _____ with him. (page 172)

5. True _____ _____ is to view everything you do, great and

   small, as an opportunity to worship God. (page 175)

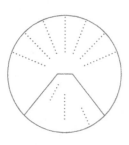

Discussion

30 MIN

1. When you set your hand to do something do you first think of the activity as an offering of worship to God? If not, what could you do to adjust your thinking?

2. Do you feel excited or intimidated when you see that the Kingdom, and by default your metron, are constantly expanding by design? Why?

3. How does viewing the world around you through the lens of reconciliation and restoration change how you do everyday life?

4. In what ways do you feel dignity and mission have been restored to your life and vocation through understanding yourself to be a Metron Manager?

NOTES

_____

_____

_____

_____

_____

_____

_____

_____

_____

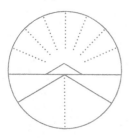

Application

20 MIN

For this activity you will be with your immediate study group members or 'Metron Council'. This activity will give participants an opportunity to bring questions before the Lord and be open with each other.

Together you will seek the Lord about anything and everything that you need help with in order to manage your metron. Remember, the manifold wisdom of God is available to His co-laborers.

METRON COUNCIL ACTIVITY

Now that you have completed this extensive study course and read *Managing Your Metron* you will have discovered much of what is in your metron and it is likely you will have questions. As we discovered in this study, the Church has access to the manifold wisdom of God! Guidance and answers are available and often these will come through other members of the body of Christ.

METRON COUNCIL ACTIVITY INSTRUCTIONS:

1. Each group member (Metron Manager) will have a total of 10 minutes to share and receive feedback from the group (Metron Council). Questions, challenges or opportunities can be shared by the metron manager to the level they are comfortable.

   Each listening group member will then respond with a brief point of input or ask clarifying questions with the aim of offering the Holy Spirit an opportunity to input into what the metron manager has shared.

2. Each metron council member should limit their response to one thought, scripture, observation, or possible solution to each question posed by the metron manager who is seeking input.

3. While each metron council member responds, listening members of the group will use a piece of paper to write down the top THREE responses that they heard being shared by the council members in response to items presented by the metron manager. They will put their name above the list of these three top responses and give the paper to the metron manager for their consideration.

4. Each metron manager should be given the chance to share a question, challenge or opportunity, hear the verbal input from each metron council member and collect all the written response papers. This process should be kept to 10 minutes per metron manager.

5. This process can be repeated as time allows so that group members can seek input from the metron council on other important questions, challenges and opportunities.

6. Evaluation: Once metron managers have shared and collected the written down top three responses from each metron council member, they will then evaluate the written responses to see if there is a trend or agreement among the various input from the group as to solutions and wisdom. Remember, the Lord is in your midst and as you go up to meet with him he will teach you his ways… then you can walk in His paths in every area of your metron. God works through his church. This is where we encounter the manifold wisdom of God.

NOTES

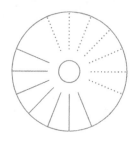

Identify your key takeaways from today's session. Your group can work together to identify their key takeaways or participants can do so individually.

1. _____

2. _____

3. _____

Takeaway
5 MIN

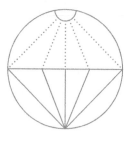

1. Pray that God would show you what He wants to bring into your metron. What expansion is He wanting you to embrace?

2. Ask God to give you wisdom and insight to know how to bring reconciliation and restoration into your metron.

3. Pray that you would not give into living as a Christian gnostic.

4. Repent if you are avoiding personal responsibility for the Kingdom and ask God how you should re-engage with your original commission and the great commission.

Prayer
10 MIN

As you work your way through this study guide, you will become more and more aware of the elements and areas that comprise your Metron. This 'Discover your Metron' worksheet is not intended to produce an exact representation of your Metron, but rather to capture your thoughts and insights as you move through this study guide and complete the reading of the book *Managing Your Metron*.

Societal

Family

Recreation

Employment

Church

Education

Managing Your Metron: A Study Guide

Scripture quotations, unless otherwise indicated, are taken from the New American Standard Bible® (NASB), Copyright ©1960, 1962, 1963, 1968, 1971, 1972, 1973,1975, 1977, 1995 by The Lockman Foundation. Used by permission. www.Lockman.org

Scripture taken from the New King James Version®. Copyright © 1982 by Thomas Nelson. Used by permission. All rights reserved.

ISBN: 978-0-578-70017-5

1st Edition, 2nd Imprint. September 2020.

Printed in the United States of America.

CPSIA information can be obtained
at www.ICGtesting.com
Printed in the USA
JSHW020109121020
8668JS00001B/1

9 780578 700175